"The Story of Blizzard and Lulu"

Jim Burris

DEDICATION

This book is dedicated to Blizzard and Lulu.

iv

In Loving Memory of Blizzard

Blizzard lived with the Mazzarella family in northwest Washington. He was a silent and shy gentle giant…anxious about new experiences. David Mazzarella had to coax Blizzard out of a puppy carrier during their first visit. Blizzard was very cautious and unsure about this new person. They began a peaceful life filled with many walks and a lot of cookies.

Jim Burris

Lulu at Mountain School

The Mazzarellas made the decision to add another furry member to their family. A 1 ½ pound , five week old Japanese Chin named Lulu. Blizzard didn't know what to think of Lulu. She was so tiny and moved very quickly. She made funny sounds and ran in circles. Lulu wandered aimlessly and Blizzard was concerned for her safety.

Jim Burris

When Lulu became tired she climbed up onto Blizzard's back. She fluffed and ruffled his fur until she made a nest. She curled up into a tiny ball and fell asleep. This happened regularly. Blizzard was very happy knowing Lulu was resting closely…very close. Blizzard's paternal instinct took over. One would think Lulu was his baby.

David has always been an animal lover and avid outdoorsman. He took Blizzard and Lulu everywhere he went. The trio wandered to the mountains and into the forest. Blizzard took his new responsibility of raising Lulu serious. He forgot about his fear and shyness.

Padilla Bay – San Juan Island

One afternoon while Blizzard and Lulu slept in their favorite position, there was a sound that awoke them. Blizzard stood up and walked to the window to investigate. Lulu stayed in her nest on his back! She was riding her best friend! Blizzard and Lulu began attracting a lot of attention. Blizzard walked while Lulu rode...a natural team. The photos and videos flowed throughout social media. They became an immediate sensation and message of love, hope and friendship.

Blizzard and Lulu

Jim Burris

Little Mountain

David isn't new to animal behavior. He began his adult life as a breeder of Chinese Shar Pei, English Bulldogs and Italian Mastiff puppies. His passion for animals grew alongside his business. During the past thirty years the Mazzarella family has cared for many types of cats, dogs, reptiles and parrots.

David declined a full athletic scholarship to a prestigious college and several lucrative opportunities so he could continue breeding and caring for puppies. Blizzard and Lulu were different. The three formed a loyal and loving team. While they enjoyed their daily adventures they were making friends internationally.

Jim Burris

Mountain School

Several years passed. Lulu was exactly what Blizzard needed…a little baby, a sister…a best friend. Lulu found the comfort and security that she missed as a newborn puppy. Outwardly, an odd couple…best friends forever.

Don't let Lulu's full grown size of four pounds fool you. She is very much in control of everything. She loves to explore, swim and ride in the kayak. She makes Blizzard aware of any boundaries he may cross.

Blizzard, at 130 pounds, has a heart filled with love and peace. Always gentle with Lulu and aware of their size difference. He took care of Lulu.

Pioneer Park

Jim Burris

Mountain School

Mountain School

Jim Burris

Washington Pass – Liberty Bell

Blizzard was growing old. His hips began to weaken. His knees started to hurt. He was slowing down. David watched closely, knowing everything would change one day.

David had many private conversations with Blizzard letting him know how much he was loved. He told Blizzard about the aging process and what to expect. David respects the elderly…human and animal. Blizzard will always have the best of care.

David told Blizzard it was fine to let go...and he was the best dog in the whole world. He reminded him of all of the adventures, the fun, the laughter and the people. The people of many cultures and diverse backgrounds that love him. Lulu Sat on Blizzard's back and listened.

Lulu knew. She watched and listened. She licked Blizzard's head as an attempt to comfort him. She walked in circles anticipating the events of the next moments.

Jim Burris

It was with great sadness and
sorrow, David continued to hug
and whisper to Blizzard. It was time.

Blizzard left the earth. He traveled
to Rainbow Bridge…where he waits
for his loving family.

Rainbow Bridge – Pioneer Park

Jim Burris

Millions of Blizzard and Lulu's
friends felt the deep emotional
pain. The last photos and videos
streamed social media. A huge loss
and seemingly the end of this true
love story.

Jim Burris

Brody and Lulu

The Mazzarellas had already decided to add another furry member to their family. Brody was 12 weeks old, also a Saint Bernard. Blizzard forged the path for another friend and companion.

Lulu, would you, please, tell me the story of Rainbow Bridge again? Sure, Brody, I'll start at the beginning…

Jim Burris

Diablo Lake

The story of Blizzard and Lulu will never end. They will live forever in the memories and hearts of many. Blizzard will always be a part of Lulu and David's story.

Thank you, Blizzard, for a lifetime of beautiful memories. You will never be forgotten.

Jim Burris

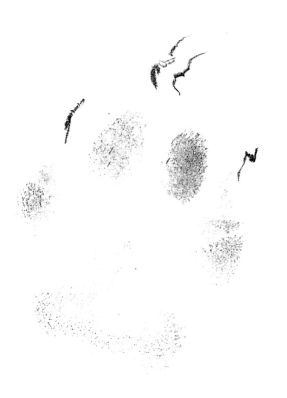

A NOTE FROM THE AUTHOR

I created these illustrations using watercolor. Beautiful reproductions are available. For information on how to purchase the 12x18 prints go to FineArtAmerica.com and search for Jim Burris.

Instagram
@jim_burris_watercolorist

Email tattoojims@gmail.com

I'll be writing and illustrating at least ten more books in this series.

53474926R00024

Made in the USA
San Bernardino, CA
18 September 2017